My 100 Must Know Learn to Write Sight Words Kindergarten Workbook

Ages 3-5

Top 100 High-Frequency Sight Words

Want Free Extra Goodies for Your Student?

Email us at: info@homerunpress.com

Title the email "My 100 Must Know Sight Words Kindergarten Workbook" and we'll send some extra worksheets your way!

We create our workbooks with love and great care.
For any issues with your workbook, such as printing errors, typos, faulty binding, or something else, please do not hesitate to contact us at:
info@homerunpress.com.
We will make sure you get a replacement copy immediately.

THANK YOU!

First published in the USA 2020.   ISBN 9781952368707

1. <u>Say</u> the word. <u>Trace</u> the word. <u>Write</u> the word.

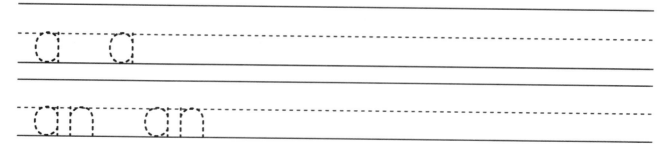

2. <u>Read</u> each sentence. <u>Write</u> the missing word ("a" or "an").

I live in __ wonderful place.

I am __ apple.

3. The word **an** is hidden **3** times on each track. <u>Find</u> them and <u>circle</u>.

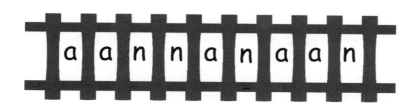

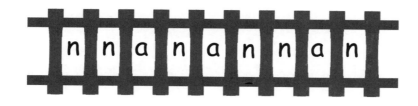

1. <u>Say</u> the word. <u>Trace</u> the word. <u>Write</u> the word.

and and

as as

2. <u>Read</u> each sentence. <u>Write</u> the missing word ("and" or "as").

I am nice _____ kind.

I am _____ tall _____ my brother.

3. Some of the words have **and** hidden inside. <u>Find</u> the words and <u>write</u> them below.

hand   fast   candy

fan   sand   man   land

www.homerunpress.com

1. <u>Say</u> the word. <u>Trace</u> the word. <u>Write</u> the word.

are are

am am

2. <u>Read</u> each sentence. <u>Write</u> the missing word (**"am"** or **"are"**).

I ____ six years old.

You _____ in my team, aren't you?

3. Here are some words that start with letter **a**. <u>Say</u> them aloud. Then <u>trace</u> each word.

are

as

and

am

are

as

and

am

1. <u>Say</u> the word. <u>Trace</u> the word. <u>Write</u> the word.

at at

all all

2. <u>Read</u> each sentence. <u>Write</u> the missing word ("at" or "all").

I ate _____ of the cupcakes.

"We are having dinner ____ home ____ six o'clock," said Mother.

3. <u>Color</u> the box that has all the words spelled correctly.

aee	are	are	are
and	ank	and	and
am	at	at	att
as	ase	as	as
al	all	all	lal

1. <u>Say</u> the word. <u>Trace</u> the word. <u>Write</u> the word.

ate ate

after after

2. <u>Read</u> each sentence. <u>Unscramble</u> the letters.

I **eta** _____ a red apple.

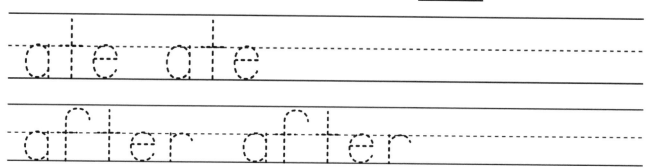

I was running **etrfa** _____ my sister.

3. <u>Find</u> each word in the word search.

all　　　　　**after**　　　　　**and**

　　are　　　　　**am**　　　　　**ate**

w g g h r a a m e k
k l w e t r k q w i
f a t u a e d g n i
r f l h t a a l a d
a q z l a t e n n e
r o x b j r d c b r

1. <u>Say</u> the word. <u>Trace</u> the word. <u>Write</u> the word.

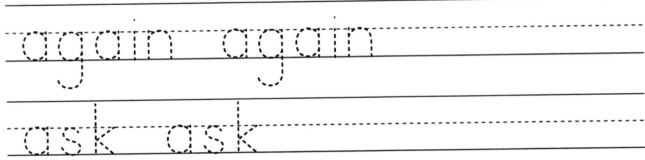

again again

ask ask

2. <u>Draw</u> a line to connect opposite words.

Antonyms are words that have opposite meanings.

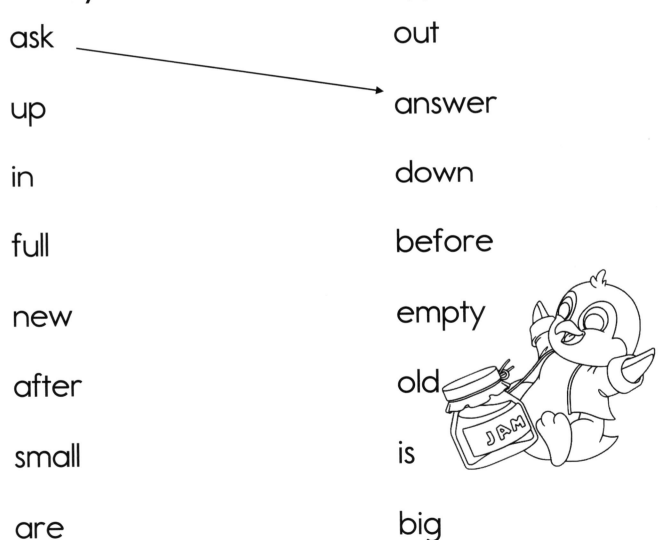

ask	out
up	answer
in	down
full	before
new	empty
after	old
small	is
are	big

www.homerunpress.com

1. <u>Say</u> the word. <u>Trace</u> the word. <u>Write</u> the word.

be   be

big   big

2. <u>Use</u> the code to find out the word. **e** = ☐   **i** = △

b ☐   _____   b △ g   _____

b ☐ ☐   _____   b △ rd   _____

3. Some of the words have **be** hidden inside. <u>Find</u> the words and <u>write</u> them below.

bee   see   bold   basket

bed   bear   bad   bell

1. <u>Say</u> the word. <u>Trace</u> the word. <u>Write</u> the word.

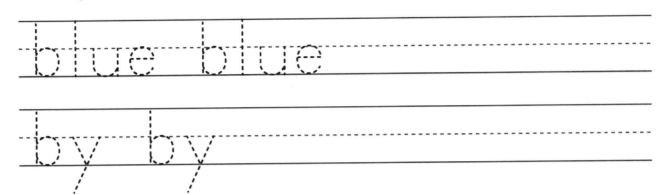

2. <u>Read</u> each sentence. <u>Write</u> the missing word ("blue" or "by").

The sky is _____.

I was hit _____ a ball.

I go to school _____ bus.

Please put the _____ crayon here.

Open the _____ book.

I like books _____ Lincoln Pierce.

I have got to read two pages _____ Monday.

This hat is _____.

1. <u>Say</u> the word. <u>Trace</u> the word. <u>Write</u> the word.

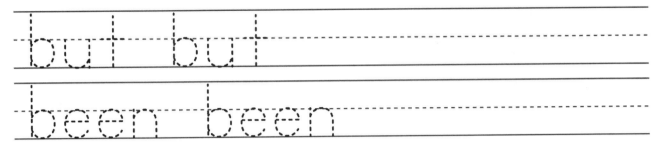

but but

been been

2. <u>Draw</u> a line to connect words that **rhyme**. <u>Say</u> the words.

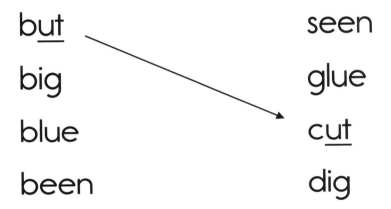

but   seen

big   glue

blue   cut

been   dig

3. <u>Draw</u> a line from the snail to the pear with the letters that finish the word **been**.

1. <u>Say</u> the word. <u>Trace</u> the word. <u>Write</u> the word.

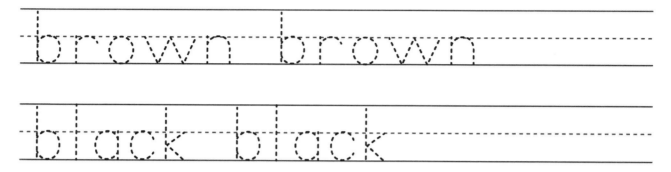

2. <u>Circle</u> the **2** errors in the sentence. <u>Write</u> the corrections above each error.

Skunk's fur comes in different patterns of

bleck end white.

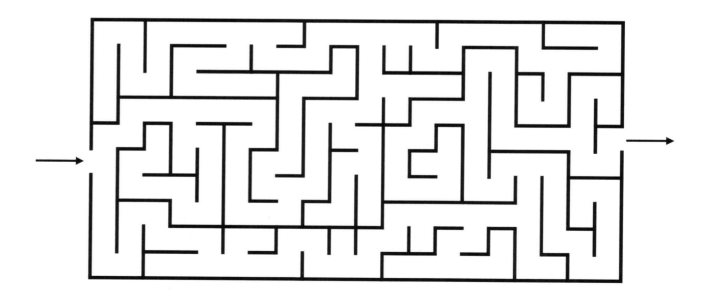

1. <u>Say</u> the word. <u>Trace</u> the word. <u>Write</u> the word.

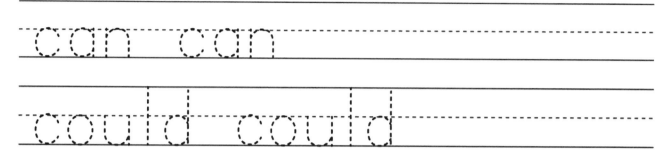

2. <u>Read</u> each sentence. <u>Write</u> the missing word ("can" or "could").

My toy _____ purr like a cat.

I _____ help you!

3. <u>Write</u> the missing letters to write the word **can** or **could**.

1. <u>Say</u> the word. <u>Trace</u> the word. <u>Write</u> the word.

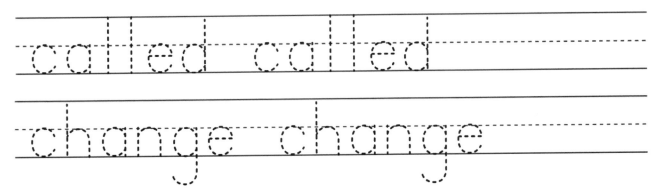

2. <u>Draw</u> a line to connect words that are the **same** or synonyms. <u>Say</u> the words.

Synonyms are words that mean exactly or almost the same.

called	big
little	high
above	cried
car	close
tall	on the top
thick	small
slam	vehicle

 www.homerunpress.com

1. <u>Say</u> the word. <u>Trace</u> the word. <u>Write</u> the word.

come come

came came

2. <u>Read</u>. <u>Write</u> the missing word (**"come" or "came"**).

The bear _____ out to eat berries.

Little Sister, _____ and dig a hole! That's fun!

3. <u>Look</u> at each box. <u>Find</u> the words whose letters fit in the boxes. <u>Write</u> the words.

brown   **come**   **change**   **could**

1. <u>Say</u> the word. <u>Trace</u> the word. <u>Write</u> the word.

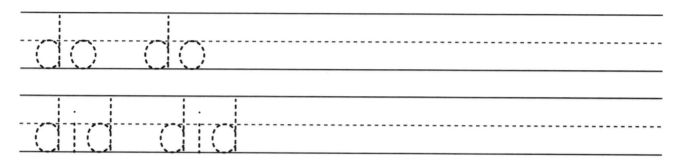

2. <u>Read</u> each sentence. <u>Write</u> the missing word (**"do"** or **"did"**).

_____ you see my sister now?

I _____ not ride my bike.

3. <u>Circle</u> the **3** errors in the story. <u>Write</u> the corrections above each error.

I du not like to play with my little brother. He breaks my toys. Hee gets mad. My Mom says that he is small, but he grows fast. He will bee my best buddy soon!

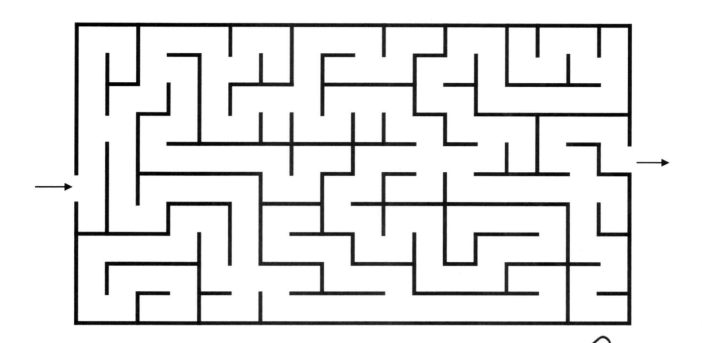

1. Find and circle or cross out the words.

E Q O B O L N B D V
C M L T B S V L N P
C U O I O D N A A Z
E C G C C G N C A L
B F E Q D I A K S K
U R R N A C X T K R
A I O G I K X O E V
J A A W A F T E R R
N E E B N A L L I N
S K F D H O L P T X

AND	ARE
COME	ALL
ATE	ASK
AGAIN	BIG
AFTER	BLUE
BROWN	BEEN
BLACK	CAN

1. <u>Say</u> the word. <u>Trace</u> the word. <u>Write</u> the word.

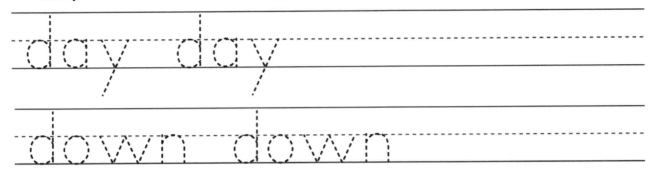

day day

down down

2. <u>Draw</u> a line to finish the sentences.

It was a beautiful   mouse.

I like to   fun.

Playing with my toys is   draw.

I saw a small furry   day.

3. <u>Color</u> the lemons with the word **day** inside.

day   may   can   day

   www.homerunpress.com

1. <u>Say</u> the word. <u>Trace</u> the word. <u>Write</u> the word.

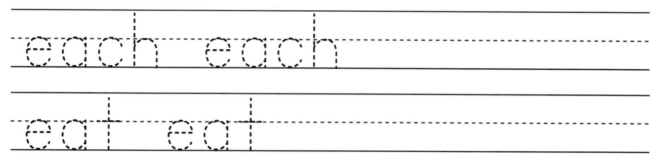

2. <u>Read</u>. <u>Write</u> the missing word (**"down," "each,"** or **"eat"**).

I walked _____ the stairs.

My dog likes to _____ berries.

_____ toy is unique!

My friend went_____ the slide.

3. The word **eat** is hidden **2** times on the track. <u>Find</u> them and <u>cross them out</u>.

1. <u>Say</u> the word. <u>Trace</u> the word. <u>Write</u> the word.

end end

every every

A *verb* is a word that *shows action.*

An *adjective* is a word that *describes a noun.*

2. <u>Circle</u> the **verb** in each sentence. <u>Underline</u> the **adjective** in each sentence.

Every kid has a special talent.

I was the first player to catch a ball.

He is sad as he cannot fly.

I like to cheer my crying sister up.

When the heavy rain ends, I will play ball.

1. <u>Say</u> the word. <u>Trace</u> the word. <u>Write</u> the word.

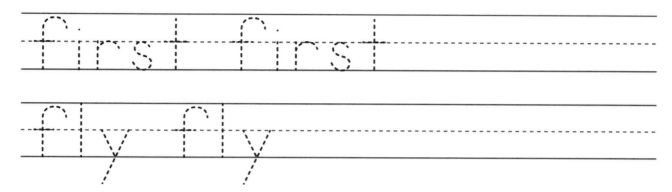

first first

fly fly

2. <u>Find</u> and <u>circle</u> or <u>cross out</u> the words.

F	T	V	E	Q	E	L
U	I	A	G	L	V	F
G	C	R	E	W	E	T
H	B	Q	S	F	R	G
Y	L	F	A	T	Y	P
Z	H	C	Z	D	I	B
K	I	M	K	A	U	P

FLY

EACH

FIRST

EAT

EVERY

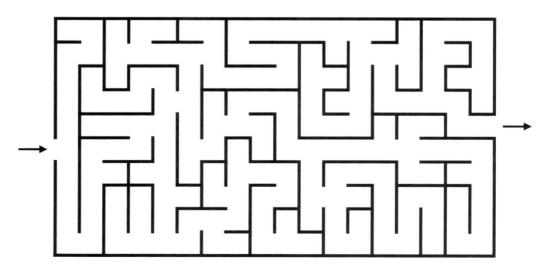

1. <u>Say</u> the word. <u>Trace</u> the word. <u>Write</u> the word.

for for

four four

2. <u>Unscramble</u> and <u>complete</u> each sentence.

This is a card _____ you.
rfo

Color _____ candies.
rofu

3. Some of the words have **for** hidden inside. <u>Find</u> the words and <u>write</u> them below.

force   **fifty**   **forty**   **fork**

_____

_____

        www.homerunpress.com

1. <u>Say</u> the word. <u>Trace</u> the word. <u>Write</u> the word.

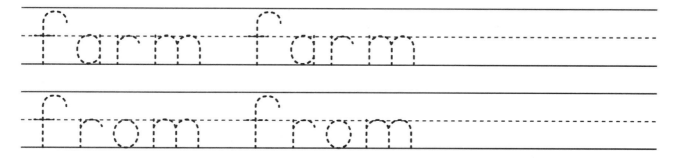

2. <u>Rewrite</u> the words in **alphabetical order**.

are   1. _____

go   2. _____

first   3. _____

big   4. _____

farm   5. _____

each   6. _____

change   7. _____

get   8. _____

from   9. _____

1. <u>Say</u> the word. <u>Trace</u> the word. <u>Write</u> the word.

get   get

go   go

2. <u>Read</u>. <u>Write</u> the missing word (**"get," "go," "see,"** or **"eat"**).

Our family likes to _____ to the fair. My

brother likes to _____ the animals. My

sister likes to _____ on a ride. I like to

_____ ice-cream. After that, we all

_____ hot dogs.

1. <u>Say</u> the word. <u>Trace</u> the word. <u>Write</u> the word.

2. <u>Read</u> the words. <u>Circle</u> **one** of the three words that **means almost the same thing as the first word.**

good

    a) bad   b) nice   c) ugly

make

    a) read   b) build   c) take

get

    a) lost   b) find   c) play

end

    a) finish   b) open   c) start

1. <u>Say</u> the word. <u>Trace</u> the word. <u>Write</u> the word.

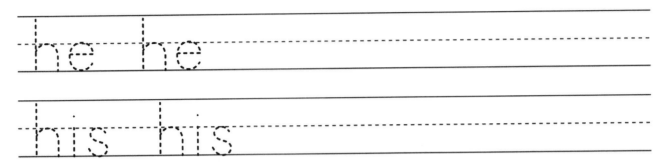

2. <u>Read</u> each sentence. <u>Write</u> the missing word (**"he"** or **"his"**).

This gnome likes to read. _____ often goes

to the library. _____ wagon is always filled

with fantasy books. _____ likes to read to

himself.   Sometimes   _____   reads   to

_____ friends.

3. Do you like to read?

_____.

1. <u>Say</u> the word. <u>Trace</u> the word. <u>Write</u> the word.

has has

have have

2. <u>Look</u> at the pictures. <u>What pictures on the page</u> begin with the letter **h**? <u>Circle</u> them and <u>write</u> each word.

sun   heart   horn   hat

elf   donut   hand   bee

1. <u>Say</u> the word. <u>Trace</u> the word. <u>Write</u> the word.

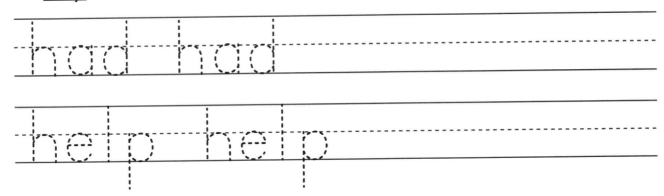

2. <u>Look</u> at the words and think about how they are related. <u>Find</u> the missing word in the list and <u>write</u> it.

first   **had**   **funny**   **give**

good   **stay**

come is to **came** as **have** is to _____

open is to **close** as **leave** is to _____

subtract is to **add** as **take** is to _____

small is to **big** as **boring** is to _____

big is to **small** as **last** is to _____

naughty is to **bad** as **nice** is to _____

1. <u>Say</u> the word. <u>Trace</u> the word. <u>Write</u> the word.

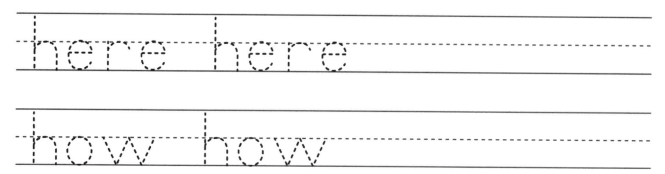

here here

how how

2. <u>Circle</u> words that need to be capitalized. <u>Write</u> the missing word (**"here" or "how"**). <u>Write</u> the corrections above each error.

You should capitalize the first word of a sentence; the pronoun I; holidays, months, and days of the week.

It rained _____ on christmas Eve,

december 24. i wondered _____ we could

celebrate christmas when it was raining.

when i asked my mom about it, she told me

to wait and see.

1. <u>Say</u> the word. <u>Trace</u> the word. <u>Write</u> the word.

her   her

him   him

2. <u>Read.</u> <u>Write</u> the missing word (**"him", "a," or "her"**).

My sister is a baby. I cannot help _____. She

needs _____ mother.

One day, _____ big dinosaur fell down from

the sky. He was green. _____ note was

attached to _____. It said, "Hi, I am _____

dinosaur!"

3. <u>Circle</u> the **3** errors in the sentence. <u>Write</u> the corrections above each error.

My brother dose not want too become an

hero.

1. <u>Find</u> and <u>circle</u> or <u>cross out</u> the words.

```
Y E J V E T D N I F        DAY      DOWN
G R A I V S G O R L        EAT      EACH
C E E C A R E O F Y        EVERY    END
T X U V H I M O Y I        FIRST    FLY
D O U J E F R N F K        FOR      FOUR
D O W N E W N F X V        FROM     FIND
V I O P Y U C O X P        FUNNY    GET
T K Y G F E Y U E E        GOOD     HAVE
S A T E G M N R D U
D W E A T R E D F J
```

1. <u>Say</u> the word. <u>Trace</u> the word. <u>Write</u> the word.

I

is is

in in

2. <u>Put</u> the fragment in the sentence.

My sister is good. At painting.

I discovered. A bright star in the sky.

 www.homerunpress.com

1. <u>Say</u> the word. <u>Trace</u> the word. <u>Write</u> the word.

2. <u>Look</u> at the words and <u>think</u> about how they are related. <u>Find</u> the missing word in the list and <u>write</u> it.

out   am   it   front

he is to **is** as **I** is to

_____

here is to **there** as **in** is to

_____

John is to **he** as **chair** is to

_____

after is to **before** as **back** is to

_____

1. <u>Say</u> the word. <u>Trace</u> the word. <u>Write</u> the word.

into into

if if

2. <u>Read</u> each sentence. <u>Write</u> the missing word ("into" or "if").

My sister's puppy ran _____ my cat.

My cat could knock him

_____ he wanted to.

3. Some of the words have **if** hidden inside. <u>Find</u> the words and <u>write</u> them below.

raft	gift	alive	life
fifth	spit	sniff	gifted

www.homerunpress.com

1. <u>Say</u> the word. <u>Trace</u> the word. <u>Write</u> the word.

idea idea

its its

2. <u>Read</u> each sentence. <u>Write</u> the missing word ("idea" or "its").

I am something you create in your mind. I am an _____.

A bird couldn't find _____ egg.

3. <u>Put</u> the fragment in the sentence.

The frog put its head. Under the water.

1. <u>Say</u> the word. <u>Trace</u> the word. <u>Write</u> the word.

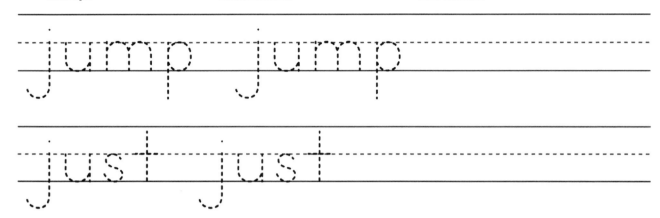

jump jump

just just

2. <u>Read</u> each sentence. <u>Unscramble</u> the word.

My brother has _____ destroyed my painting.
sutj

My sister loves to _____.
pujm

3. <u>Color</u> the box that has all the words spelled correctly.

idia	idea	ider	idea
just	jast	just	just
jumb	jump	jump	jump
into	intu	ento	into
rehe	heer	here	here

1. <u>Say</u> the word. <u>Trace</u> the word. <u>Write</u> the word.

like like

look look

2. <u>Read</u> the words. <u>Circle</u> **one** of the three words that means **the opposite of the first word.**

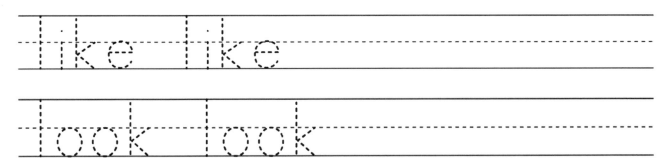

sit

a) watch   b) see   c) stand

like

a) hate   b) love   c) enjoy

hard

a) difficult   b) tough   c) easy

end

a) finish   b) stop   c) begin

1. <u>Say</u> the word. <u>Trace</u> the word. <u>Write</u> the word.

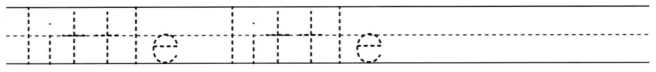

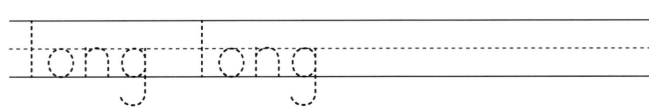

2. <u>Use</u> the code to write the word.

   www.homerunpress.com

1. <u>Say</u> the word. <u>Trace</u> the word. <u>Write</u> the word.

me me

my my

2. <u>Read</u> each sentence. <u>Unscramble</u> the letters.

What _____ I _____ to _____
          anc   igve   ym

Mom for Christmas?

A coloring _____ would be a _____
              bkoo   icen

_____.
 tifg

You _____ _____ flowers, too.
    nac   etg

1. <u>Say</u> the word. <u>Trace</u> the word. <u>Write</u> the word.

many many

more more

2. <u>Find</u> each word in the word search.

FIRST   JUST   DOWN   COME

BROWN   BLACK   DAY   FARM

END   LONG

B R O W N L O N G

H K C A L B D N E

D O W N K W H E T

S P T S R I F S Y

F A R M P Y U M A

E M O C Y J M S D

1. <u>Say</u> the word. <u>Trace</u> the word. <u>Write</u> the word.

make make

made made

2. <u>Read</u>. <u>Write</u> the missing word ("make," "made," "many," or "more").

Verb tenses tell **WHEN** the *action takes place.*

Present tense expresses action or state in the **present time:**

I want to _____ this cookie.

Do you want _____ cookies?

Yes, I'd like _____.

Past tense is what happened:

How _____ cookies did you have?

Last time, I _____ ginger cookies

1. <u>Say</u> the word. <u>Trace</u> the word. <u>Write</u> the word.

may _may_

must _must_

2. <u>Write</u> the missing word.

MAY expresses a possibility.

Must expresses a strong certainty.

Pandas _____ live in places where

bamboo plants grow.

Lions _____ sleep up to 20 hours a day.

A mouse _____ eat any kind of cheese.

Before you begin to exercise, you

_____ stretch your muscles.

I _____ go to bed at 9 pm.

1. <u>Say</u> the word. <u>Trace</u> the word. <u>Write</u> the word.

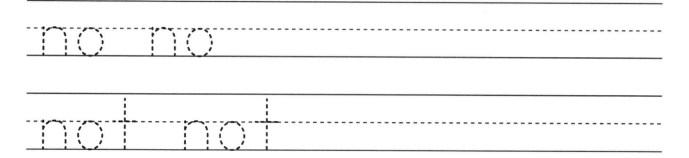

2. <u>Color</u> the clouds with the words that **rhyme with not**.

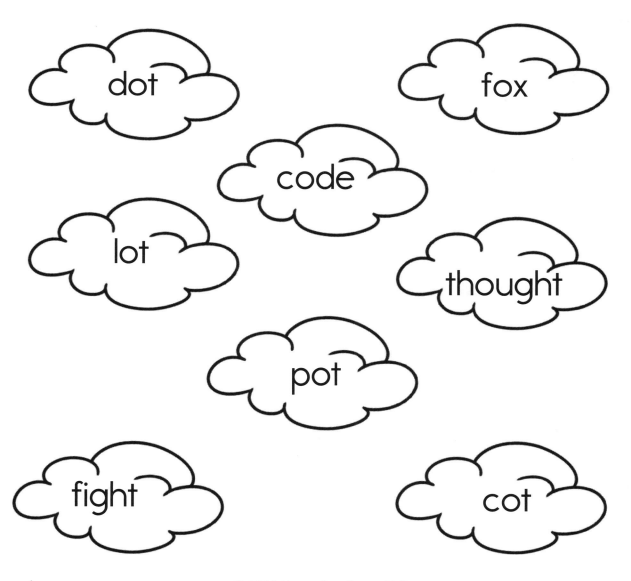

1. <u>Say</u> the word. <u>Trace</u> the word. <u>Write</u> the word.

now now

number number

2. <u>Read</u> the words. <u>Circle</u> **one** of the three words that **means the opposite of the first word.**

thick

a) lazy   b) tall   c) thin

3. <u>Unscramble</u> the words.

rmuneb   tums

verye   kema

1. <u>Say</u> the word. <u>Trace</u> the word. <u>Write</u> the word.

name name

new new

2. <u>Read</u> the words. <u>Circle</u> **one** of the three words that **means the opposite of the first word.**

new

a) dirty   b) clean   c) old

3. <u>Color</u> the clouds with the words that **rhyme with name.**

1. Find and circle or cross out the words.

```
J D Y R R J Y E L W
F U Y U E A D I V W
U Q M H B A K O O L
G E M P M E M O R E
E N L A U I D E A J
K M O T N O Z O N U
A U N L T Y J A U S
M S C N C I M D I T
G T I P D E L Y A M
W Z N G A I J K A J
```

INTO	IDEA
JUMP	JUST
LIKE	LOOK
LONG	LITTLE
MAKE	MADE
MORE	MANY
MAY	MUST
NUMBER	NAME

www.homerunpress.com

1. <u>Say</u> the word. <u>Trace</u> the word. <u>Write</u> the word.

off off

on on

2. <u>Draw</u> a line to connect the *synonyms.*

Synonyms are words that have **the same or almost the same meanings.**

off	fall
want	cute
mad	make
pretty	clever
on	onto
build	away
autumn	angry
smart	wish

1. <u>Say</u> the word. <u>Trace</u> the word. <u>Write</u> the word.

one one

our our

2. <u>Write</u> the **antonyms** in the blank

full	one	close	our
summer	like	lost	ask

their

winter

open

found

many

empty

answer

hate

1. <u>Say</u> the word. <u>Trace</u> the word. <u>Write</u> the word.

old old

out out

2. <u>Write</u> the missing words (**"old," "out," "on," "off," "of," and "inside"**).

Pumpkin carving is an _____ but enjoyable activity. Spread a piece of paper _____ _____ a table. Draw a circle around the pumpkin's stem and a creepy face _____ your pumpkin. Cut _____ the lid and scoop all _____ the seeds _____ _____ the pumpkin. Cut _____ the face and place a candle _____ your pumpkin!

1. <u>Say</u> the word. <u>Trace</u> the word. <u>Write</u> the word.

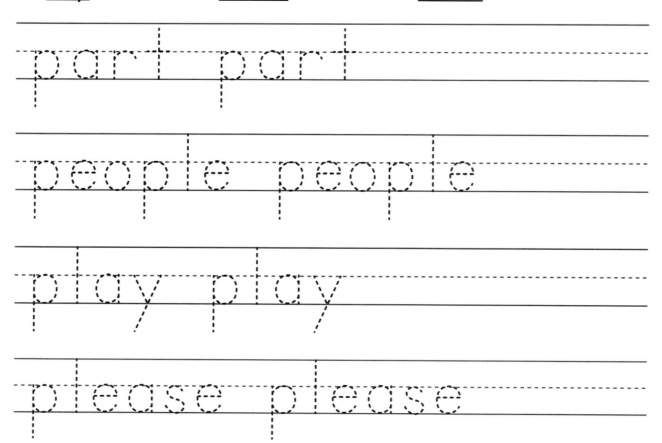

part part

people people

play play

please please

2. <u>Look</u> at each box. <u>Find</u> the words whose letters fit in the boxes. <u>Write</u> the words.

please   **people**   **part**   **play**

       www.homerunpress.com

1. <u>Use</u> the words from the choice box to <u>unscramble</u> the words below.

part	alone	doctor
coat	cake	play
key	bike	people

cato   _____

lyap   _____

rtpa   _____

oelepp   _____

iekb   _____

aoenl   _____

yke   _____

crodot   _____

ckea   _____

1. <u>Say</u> the word. <u>Trace</u> the word. <u>Write</u> the word.

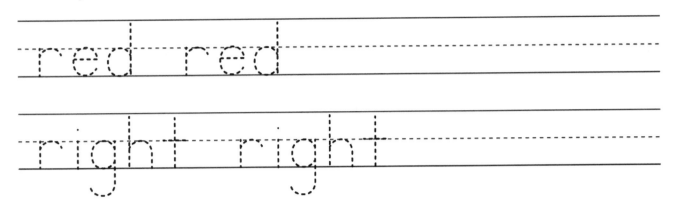

red   red

right right

2. <u>Write</u> the words in alphabetical order from a-z.

ran   1. _____

make   2. _____

say   3. _____

right   4. _____

after   5. _____

part   6. _____

new   7. _____

little   8. _____

ball   9. _____

1. <u>Say</u> the word. <u>Trace</u> the word. <u>Write</u> the word.

ran ran

run run

2. <u>Read</u>. <u>Write</u> the missing word (**"ran"** or **"run"**).

Bears do not like to _____.

The rabbit _____ with a blinding speed yesterday.

My cat _____ and chases anything that moves.

Tigers are too big to _____ after the animals.

Last week, the foxes _____ in circles to fool an enemy.

1. <u>Say</u> the word. <u>Trace</u> the word. <u>Write</u> the word.

read read

ride ride

2. <u>Read</u> the words. <u>Circle</u> **one** of the three words that **means the opposite of the first word.**

right

a) good   b) left   c) back

read

a) help   b) write   c) bake

dark

a) full   b) soft   c) light

true

a) right   b) correct   c) false

www.homerunpress.com

1. <u>Say</u> the word. <u>Trace</u> the word. <u>Write</u> the word.

sad sad

she she

2. <u>Say</u> the word. <u>Write</u> the word, using the **past tense** of the underlined word in the first sentence.

caught   read   played

My sister likes to <u>read</u>.

Last time, she _____ a fantasy book.

My cat loves to <u>play</u> with a ball.

Last time, it _____ with a ball.

A frog <u>catches</u> flies with its tongue.

Yesterday, a frog _____ a fly with its tongue.

1. <u>Say</u> the word. <u>Trace</u> the word. <u>Write</u> the word.

so so

some some

2. <u>Read</u> the words. <u>Circle</u> **one** of the three words that **means the same or almost the same as the first word.**

home

a) field   b) lake   c) house

later

a) then   b) earlier   c) now

some

a) none   b) one   c) any

cold

a) hot   b) warm   c) cool

                   www.homerunpress.com

1. <u>Say</u> the word. <u>Trace</u> the word. <u>Write</u> the word.

$\text{see} \quad \text{see}$

$\text{saw} \quad \text{saw}$

2. <u>Say</u> the word. <u>Write</u> the word, using **the past tense** of the underlined word in the first sentence.

The dog cannot <u>see</u> clearly through his long thick hair.

I _____ a snake and I was so scared!

Did you <u>see</u> my favorite book?

I _____ mine under the table.

Can you <u>see</u> a star?

I _____ a twinkling star in the sky.

I <u>see</u> a bird in the tree.

I _____ one yesterday.

1. <u>Say</u> the word. <u>Trace</u> the word. <u>Write</u> the word.

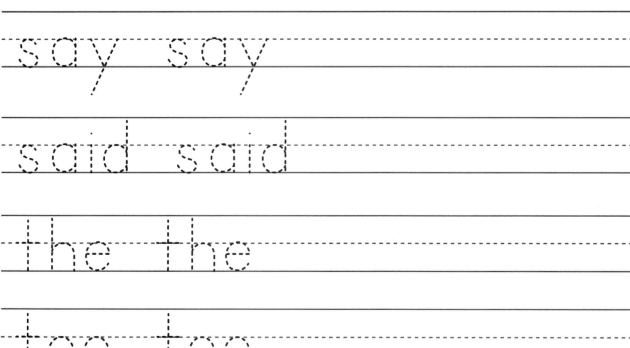

say say

said said

the the

too too

2. <u>Look</u> at each box. <u>Find</u> the words whose letters fit in the boxes. <u>Write</u> the words.

tongue　　**sister**　　**pretty**　　**loves**

© 2020 Home Run Press, LLC　　www.homerunpress.com

1. The words are mixed up. <u>Rewrite</u> each sentence in the correct order. <u>Beware</u> to use capital letters!

Capitalize the first word of the sentence!

Capitalize names and proper nouns!

sun is the big star a.

_____

has the to earth air breathe.

_____

moon the no one on lives.

_____

1. <u>Find</u> and <u>circle</u> or <u>cross out</u> the words.

E A D L P L R O Y O
X H A V X I I Q U R
W S S P G O N E E R
P C Y H I K M D Z Q
O L T P E O P L E K
T W E Y S T E E C X
H F N A A E R D X E
E N U R S L W I O A
R T R A P E P R L W
O I F X Y T D N D Z

ONE	OTHER
OUR	OLD
PART	PEOPLE
PLAY	PLEASE
RED	RIGHT
RUN	SHE
SAD	RIDE
SOME	SEE

1. <u>Say</u> the word. <u>Trace</u> the word. <u>Write</u> the word.

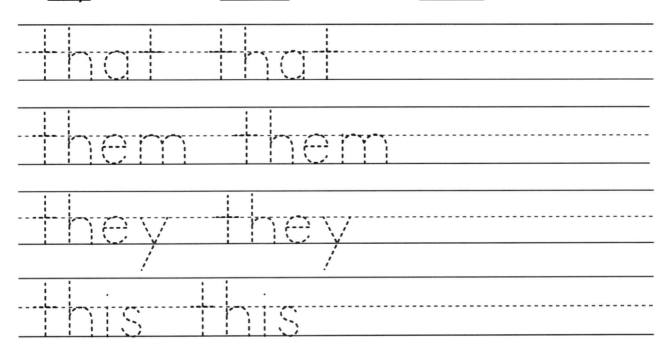

2. <u>Color</u> the clouds with the word **this** in them blue.

<u>Circle</u> the clouds with the word **that** in them.

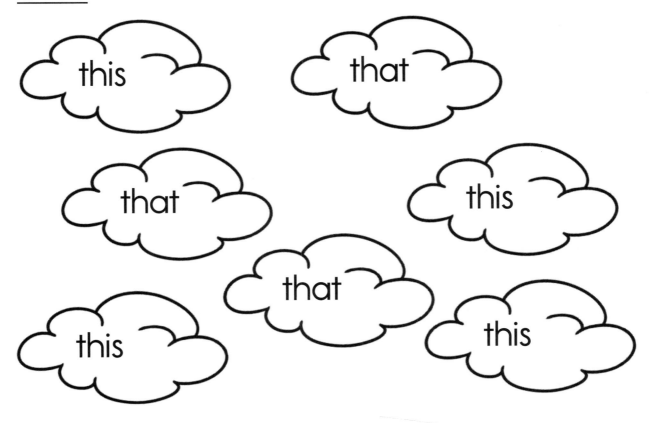

© 2020 Home Run Press, LLC

1. <u>Read.</u> <u>Write</u> the missing word (**"this," "that," "they," or "them"**). <u>Use</u> the missing quotation marks.

Use quotation marks (":…") at the beginning and end of a direct speech (words of the speaker).

He said, "My favorite Pokemon is Pikachu."

Use a comma to separate the speaker

Punctuation marks go inside the quotation marks

My brother said   I want _____ blue cupcake. _____ are my favorites.

My sister said   I want _____ cupcake. What are blue cupcakes made of? I have never tried _____.

1. <u>Say</u> the word. <u>Trace</u> the word. <u>Write</u> the word.

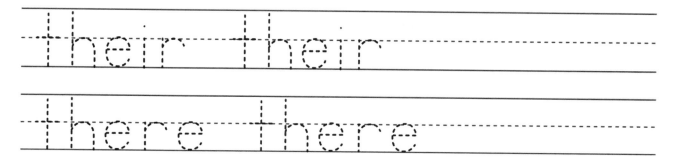

2. <u>Read</u>. <u>Circle</u> the correct homophone.

Homophones are words that you spell differently but they sound the same and have different meanings.

My friend is standing over their - there.

The scarecrow is standing over their – there house.

My bike's brake - break is broken.

My little sister likes to brake – break my toys.

I'm going to see – sea my Grandma.

See - Sea water tastes salty.

1. <u>Say</u> the word. <u>Trace</u> the word. <u>Write</u> the word.

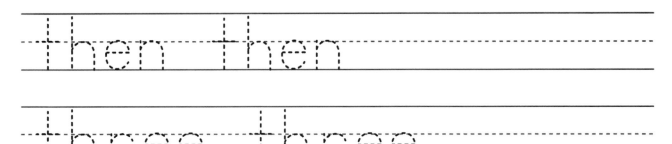

2. <u>Draw</u> a line to connect **homophones**. <u>Say</u> the words.

see	sun
here	tail
tale	poor
their	knight
right	our
night	sea
pour	hear
son	write
hour	there

1. <u>Say</u> the word. <u>Trace</u> the word. <u>Write</u> the word.

than than

these these

time time

two two

2. <u>Read</u> each sentence. <u>Practice</u> writing the word.

There are some people who are over 8 feet tall. _____ people are called giants.

The _____ is 5:30 pm.

_____ plus _____ equals four.

The chocolate cupcake is bigger _____ the strawberry cupcake.

1. <u>Read</u> each sentence. <u>Circle</u> if it is **fact or opinion.**

Fact can be proved to be true.

Ten is written as 10.

Opinion is what you think or how you feel about something.

A fantasy book is the best Christmas gift.

The Sun is made of very hot gases.

Fact

Opinion

The best place to live is near an ocean.

Fact

Opinion

The Romans hd hundreds of gods.

Fact

Opinion

www.homerunpress.com

1. <u>Say</u> the word. <u>Trace</u> the word. <u>Write</u> the word.

up up

use use

2. <u>Read</u> each sentence.

<u>Use</u> *a question mark to end a sentence that shows a direct question.* <u>Use</u> *a period to end a telling sentence.*

When do skunks use their terrible smell____

A baby kangaroo hides in its mother's pouch after it is born____

How long can camels go without food or water____

Why do birds build nests____

Which insect has a sting in its tail____

Do elephants like to be in water____

1. <u>Say</u> the word. <u>Trace</u> the word. <u>Write</u> the word.

with with

word word

2. <u>Read</u> each sentence.

<u>Use</u> *an exclamation mark (!) to end a sentence that shows excitement.*

I am scared_____

I love my new Pokemon card_____

"Wow_____" yells my sister.

I saw a twinkling star_____

There is a mouse in my room_____

Thank you for your Christmas gift_____

Stop pulling my hair_____

That's amazing_____

Wow, look at that_____

1. <u>Say</u> the word. <u>Trace</u> the word. <u>Write</u> the word.

want want

was was

we we

were were

2. <u>Look</u> at each box. <u>Find</u> the words whose letters fit in the boxes. <u>Write</u> the words.

father   mouse   want   mother

1. <u>Read</u> each word.

<u>Circle</u> *the pronouns (words that can take the place of a noun: my brother = he).*

<u>Underline</u> *the verbs (words that show action: write, learn).*

<u>Write</u> the words in alphabetical order from a-z.

I

want

you

we

am

was

she

it

use

say

he

1. _____

2. _____

3. _____

4. _____

5. _____

6. _____

7. _____

8. _____

9. _____

10. _____

11. _____

www.homerunpress.com

1. <u>Say</u> the word. <u>Trace</u> the word. <u>Write</u> the word.

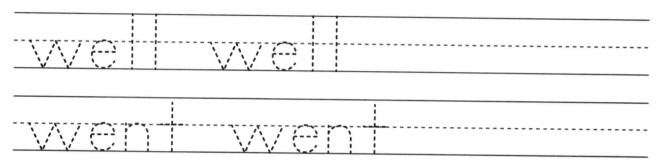

2. <u>Read</u> each sentence. <u>Write</u> the missing word ("well" or "went").

We _____ to the park.

My sister plays soccer very _____.

3. <u>Color</u> the clouds with the word **well** in them yellow.

<u>Circle</u> the clouds with the word **went** in them.

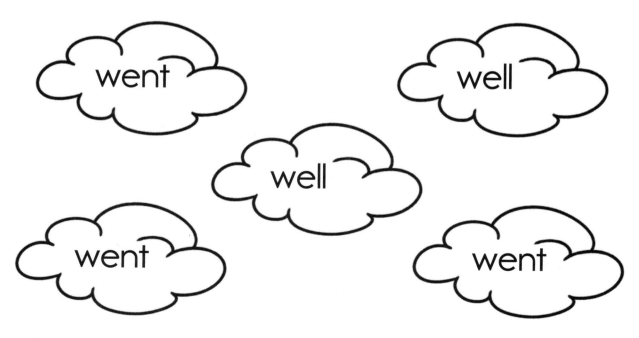

1. <u>Say</u> the word. <u>Trace</u> the word. <u>Write</u> the word.

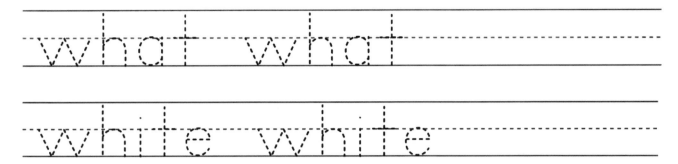

2. <u>Cross out</u> all the lemons that **don't** show the word **what**. <u>Circle</u> all the lemons that **don't** show the word **white**.

1. <u>Say</u> the word. <u>Trace</u> the word. <u>Write</u> the word.

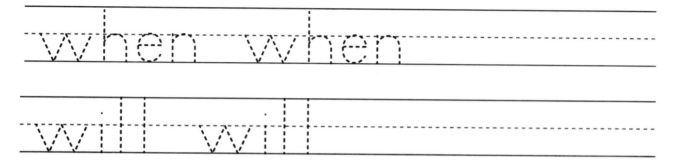

2. <u>Read</u>. <u>Write</u> the missing word (**"when" or "will"**).

_____ _____ you make a card for your friend?

The clouds _____ be made _____ many droplets of water are pushed together.

3. <u>Circle</u> the lemon with the word **when**.

1. <u>Say</u> the word. <u>Trace</u> the word. <u>Write</u> the word.

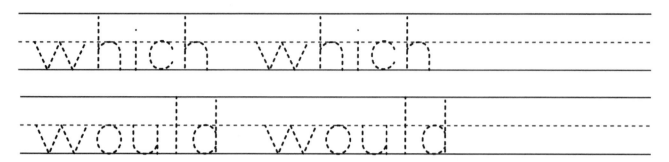

2. <u>Read</u>. <u>Unscramble</u> the missing words.

Circle *a verb (a word that shows an action)* in each sentence.

_____ cupcake do you want?

hicwh

I _____ rather have vanilla than

odwlu

chocolate cupcake.

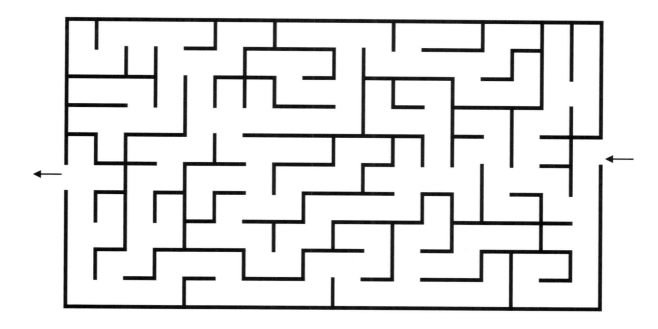

1. <u>Find</u> and <u>circle</u> or <u>cross out</u> the words.

W	H	I	C	H	E	U	T	Q	T
Q	Z	N	D	O	W	S	H	X	N
E	E	R	H	T	S	E	E	W	A
B	U	W	I	E	D	I	Y	H	W
L	A	M	T	C	R	O	T	E	T
S	E	I	H	T	O	W	H	E	N
Y	H	C	T	T	W	N	A	H	T
W	Y	A	G	H	I	O	A	B	S
N	H	Z	I	S	I	W	G	Y	I
W	K	J	D	B	F	S	W	V	U

THIS	THEY
THREE	THESE
TIME	TWO
USE	THAN
WITH	WORDS
WANT	WAS
WHAT	WHITE
WHICH	WHEN

1. <u>Say</u> the word. <u>Trace</u> the word. <u>Write</u> the word.

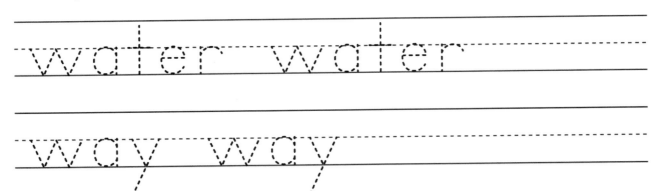

2. <u>Unscramble</u> the compound word.

The **compound** word is formed when two or more words are put together.

otof + llab

_____

two teams carry, kick, or trow
the ball on a big field of grass

tarwe + krpa

_____

an area with water slides
and swimming pools

panit + burhs

_____

used to put paint on things

 www.homerunpress.com

1. <u>Say</u> the word. <u>Trace</u> the word. <u>Write</u> the word.

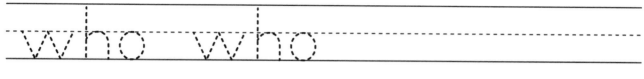

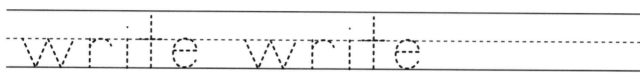

2. <u>Use</u> the code to find out the word.

ß = w   Ō = i   £ = e

Â = t   Ǿ = o   ∞ = h

n £ s Â   _____

∞ Ō l l   _____

ß ∞ Ǿ   _____

ß £ £ p   _____

ß r Ō Â £   _____

l Ō n £ s   _____

f l Ǿ ß £ r   _____

1. <u>Say</u> the word. <u>Trace</u> the word. <u>Write</u> the word.

yes   yes

you   you

2. <u>Write</u> the best antonym from the choice box.

yes	wet	tiny	full
night	sick	stay	old

day   _____

empty   _____

large   _____

leave   _____

dry   _____

no   _____

well   _____

new   _____

     www.homerunpress.com

1

My 100 Must Know Learn to Write Sight Words Kindergarten Workbook Ages 3-5

1. Say the word. Trace the word. Write the word.

an an

2. Read each sentence. Write the missing word ("a" or "an").

I live in a wonderful place.

I am an apple.

3. The word an is hidden 3 times on each track. Find them and circle.

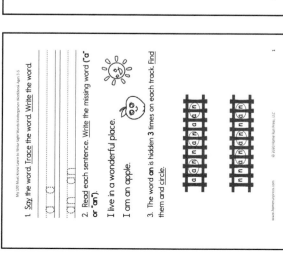

www.homerunpress.com   © 2020 Home Run Press, LLC   1

2

My 100 Must Know Learn to Write Sight Words kindergarten Workbook Ages 3-5

1. Say the word. Trace the word. Write the word.

and and

as as

2. Read each sentence. Write the missing word ("and" or "as").

I am nice and kind.

I am as tall as my brother.

3. Some of the words have and hidden inside. Find the words and write them below.

hand   fast   candy

fan   sand   man   land

hand, candy, sand, land

© 2020 Home Run Press, LLC   www.homerunpress.com   2

3

My 100 Must Know Learn to Write Sight Words kindergarten Workbook Ages 3-5

1. Say the word. Trace the word. Write the word.

are are

am am

2. Read each sentence. Write the missing word ("am" or "are").

I am six years old.

You are in my team, aren't you?

3. Here are some words that start with letter a. Say them aloud. Then trace each word.

are

as

and

am

© 2020 Home Run Press, LLC   3

4

My 100 Must Know Learn to Write Sight Words Kindergarten Workbook Ages 3-5

1. Say the word. Trace the word. Write the word.

at at

all all

2. Read each sentence. Write the missing word ("at" or "all").

I ate all of the cupcakes.

"We are having dinner at home at six o'clock," said Mother.

3. Color the box that has all the words spelled correctly.

aee	are	are
and	ank	and
am	at	att
as	ase	as
al	all	lal

www.homerunpress.com   © 2020 Home Run Press, LLC   4

5

My 100 Must Know Learn to Write Sight Words kindergarten Workbook Ages 3-5

1. Say the word. Trace the word. Write the word.

ate ate

after after

2. Read each sentence. Unscramble the letters.

I eta ate a red apple.

I was running etrfa after my sister.

3. Find each word in the word search.

all   after   and

are   am   ate

```
w g g h f g q m e k
k l w e t k q w i
f u a e d g n i
r a h t a a l a d
q z a t e m n e
r o x b j r d c b r
```

www.homerunpress.com   © 2020 Home Run Press, LLC   5

6

My 100 Must Know Learn to Write Sight Words kindergarten Workbook Ages 3-5

1. Say the word. Trace the word. Write the word.

again again

ask ask

2. Draw a line to connect opposite words.

Antonyms are words that have opposite meanings.

ask   out
up   answer
in   down
full   before
new   empty
after   old
small   is
are   big

© 2020 Home Run Press, LLC   6

7

My 100 Must Know Learn to Write Sight Words kindergarten Workbook Ages 3-5

1. Say the word. Trace the word. Write the word.

be be

big big

2. Use the code to find out the word.   e = □   i = △

b□ be   b△g   big
b□ bee   b△rd bird

3. Some of the words have be hidden inside. Find the words and write them below.

bee   see   bold   basket

bed   bear   bad   bell

bee, bed, bear, bell

www.homerunpress.com   © 2020 Home Run Press, LLC   7

8

My 100 Must Know Learn to Write Sight Words kindergarten Workbook Ages 3-5

1. Say the word. Trace the word. Write the word.

blue blue

by by

2. Read each sentence. Write the missing word ("blue" or "by").

The sky is blue.

I was hit by a ball.

I go to school by bus.

Please put the blue crayon here.

Open the blue book.

I like books by Lincoln Pierce.

I have got to read two pages by Monday.

This hat is blue.

© 2020 Home Run Press, LLC   8

Page 12

1. <u>Say</u> the word. <u>Trace</u> the word. <u>Write</u> the word.

called called

change change

2. <u>Draw</u> a line to connect words that are the **same** or **synonyms**. <u>Say</u> the words. **Synonyms are words that mean exactly or almost the same.**

called	big
little	high
above	cried
car	close
tall	on the top
thick	small
slam	vehicle

© 2020 Home Run Press, LLC

Page 11

1. Say the word. <u>Trace</u> the word. <u>Write</u> the word.

can can

could could

2. <u>Read</u> each sentence. <u>Write</u> the missing word ("can" or "could").

My toy can purr like a cat.

I could help you!

3. <u>Write</u> the missing letters to write the word **can** or **could**.

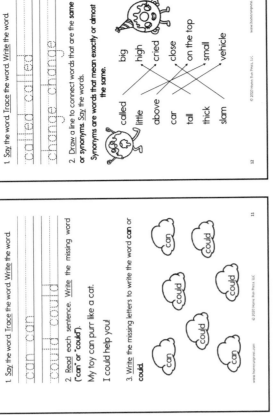

© 2020 Home Run Press, LLC

Page 10

1. <u>Say</u> the word. <u>Trace</u> the word. <u>Write</u> the word.

brown brown

black black

2. <u>Circle</u> the **2** errors in the sentence. Write the corrections above each error.

Skunk's fur comes in different patterns of black and white.

© 2020 Home Run Press, LLC

Page 9

1. <u>Say</u> the word. <u>Trace</u> the word. <u>Write</u> the word. <u>Say</u> the word.

but but

been been

2. <u>Draw</u> a line to connect words that **rhyme**. <u>Say</u> the words.

but	seen
big	glue
blue	cut
been	dig

3. <u>Draw</u> a line from the snail to the pear with the letters that finish the word **been**.

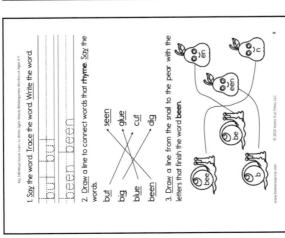

www.homerunpress.com   © 2020 Home Run Press, LLC

Page 16

1. <u>Say</u> the word. <u>Trace</u> the word. <u>Write</u> the word.

day day

down down

2. <u>Draw</u> a line to finish the sentences.

It was a beautiful   mouse.

I like to   fun.

Playing with my toys is   draw.

I saw a small furry   day.

3. <u>Color</u> the lemons with the word **day** inside.

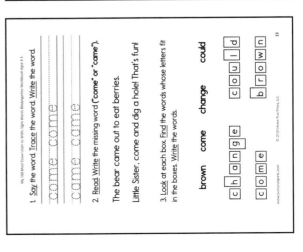

© 2020 Home Run Press, LLC

Page 15

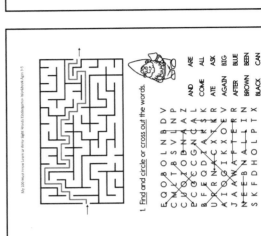

1. <u>Find</u> and <u>circle</u> or <u>cross out</u> the words.

```
E Q O B O L N B D V
C N L T B S V L N Z
C U O T O D N A A Z
P C G E C G N C A L
B F E Q D I A R S K
U P R N A C X T K R
A I O G I K X O E V
J A A W F T E R R R
N E E B N A L L I N
S K F D H O L P T X
```

AND	ARE	ALL
COME	ATE	ASK
AGAIN	AFTER	BIG
BROWN	BLUE	
BLACK	BEEN	CAN

www.homerunpress.com   © 2020 Home Run Press, LLC

Page 14

1. <u>Say</u> the word. <u>Trace</u> the word. <u>Write</u> the word.

do do

did did

2. <u>Read</u> each sentence. <u>Write</u> the missing word ("do" or "did").

Do you see my sister now?

I did not ride my bike.

3. <u>Circle</u> the **3** errors in the story. <u>Write</u> the corrections above each error.

I do not like to play with my little brother. He breaks my toys. He gets mad. My Mom says that he is small, but he grows fast. He will be my best buddy soon!

www.homerunpress.com   © 2020 Home Run Press, LLC

Page 13

1. <u>Say</u> the word. <u>Trace</u> the word. <u>Write</u> the word.

come come

came came

2. <u>Read</u> <u>Write</u> the missing word ("come" or "came").

The bear came out to eat berries.

Little Sister, come and dig a hole! That's fun!

3. <u>Look</u> at each box. <u>Find</u> the words whose letters fit in the boxes. <u>Write</u> the words.

brown   come   change   could

c	h	a	n	g	e		c	o	u	l	d

c	o	m	e		b	r	o	w	n

www.homerunpress.com   © 2020 Home Run Press, LLC

17

1. Say the word. Trace the word. Write the word.

   each each

   eat eat

2. Read. Write the missing word ("down," "each," or "eat").

   I walked down the stairs.

   My dog likes to eat berries.

   Each toy is unique!

   My friend went down the slide.

3. The word **eat** is hidden **2** times on the track. Find them and cross them out.

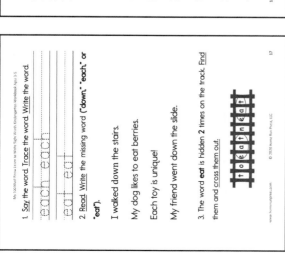

www.homerunpress.com   © 2020 Home Run Press, LLC   17

18

1. Say the word. Trace the word. Write the word.

   and end

   every every

A verb is a word that shows action.

An adjective is a word that describes a noun.

2. Circle the **verb** in each sentence. Underline the **adjective** in each sentence.

   Every kid (has) a special talent.

   I (was) the first player to (catch) a ball.

   He (is) sad as he (cannot fly)

   I (like) to (cheer) my crying sister up.

   When the heavy rain ends, I (will play) ball.

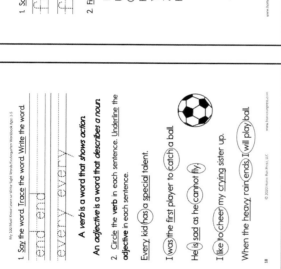

18

19

1. Say the word. Trace the word. Write the word.

   first first

   fly fly

2. Find and circle or cross out the words.

   F T V E Q E L   FLY
   U I X G L Y T   EACH
   G C R E W E T   FIRST
   H B Q S F R G   EAT
   Y L F A T Y P   EVERY
   Z H C Z D I B
   K I M K A U P

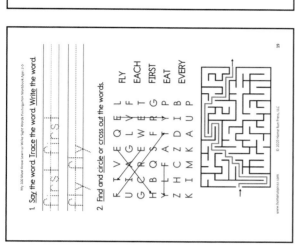
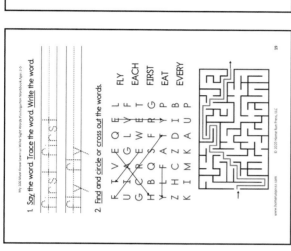

www.homerunpress.com   © 2020 Home Run Press, LLC   19

20

1. Say the word. Trace the word. Write the word.

   for for

   four four

2. Unscramble and complete each sentence.

   This is a card for ____ you.   rfo

   Color four ____ candies.   rofu

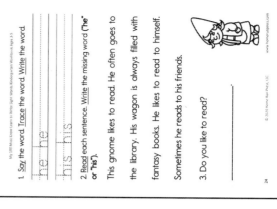

3. Some of the words have **for** hidden inside. Find the words and write them below.

   force   fifty   forty   fork

   force, forty, fork

© 2020 Home Run Press, LLC   20

21

1. Say the word. Trace the word. Write the word.

   farm farm

   from from

2. Rewrite the words in alphabetical order.

are	1. are
go	2. big
first	3. change
big	4. each
farm	5. farm
each	6. first
change	7. from
get	8. get
from	9. go

www.homerunpress.com   © 2020 Home Run Press, LLC   21

22

1. Say the word. Trace the word. Write the word.

   get get

   go go

2. Read. Write the missing word ("get," "go," "see," or "eat").

   Our family likes to go to the fair. My brother

   likes to go to see the animals. My sister likes to go

   on a ride. I like to get ice-cream. After that,

   we all eat hot dogs.

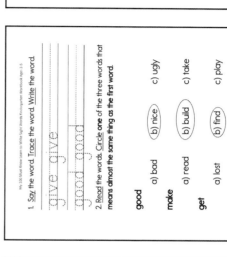

22

23

1. Say the word. Trace the word. Write the word.

   give give

   good good

2. Read the words. Circle **one** of the three words that means almost **the same thing as the first word.**

   good   a) bad   b) nice   c) ugly

   make   a) read   b) build   c) take

   get   a) lost   b) find   c) play

   end   a) finish   b) open   c) start

www.homerunpress.com   © 2020 Home Run Press, LLC   23

24

1. Say the word. Trace the word. Write the word.

   he he

   his his

2. Read each sentence. Write the missing word ("he" or "his").

   This gnome likes to read. He often goes to

   the library. His wagon is always filled with

   fantasy books. He likes to read to himself.

   Sometimes he reads to his friends.

3. Do you like to read?

   _____

© 2020 Home Run Press, LLC   24

25

1. <u>Say</u> the word. <u>Trace</u> the word. <u>Write</u> the word.

has has

have have

2. <u>Look</u> at the pictures. <u>What</u> pictures on the page begin with the letter h? <u>Circle</u> them and <u>write</u> each word.

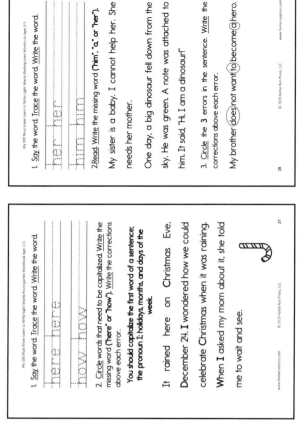

sun   heart   hat

elf   donut   bee

heart, horn, hat, hand

26

1. <u>Say</u> the word. <u>Trace</u> the word. <u>Write</u> the word.

had had

help help

2. <u>Look</u> at the words and think about how they are related. <u>Find</u> the missing word in the list and <u>write</u> it.

first   had   funny   give

good   stay

come is to **came** as **have** is to _____   had

open is to **close** as **leave** is to _____   stay

subtract is to **add** as **take** is to _____   give

small is to **big** as **boring** is to _____   funny

big is to **small** as **last** is to _____   first

naughty is to **bad** as **nice** is to _____   good

27

1. <u>Say</u> the word. <u>Trace</u> the word. <u>Write</u> the word.

here here

now now

2. <u>Circle</u> words that need to be capitalized. <u>Write</u> the missing word (**"here"** or **"now"**). <u>Write</u> the corrections above each error.

You should capitalize the first word of a sentence; the pronoun I; holidays, months, and days of the week.

It rained here on Christmas Eve.

December 24, I wondered how we could celebrate Christmas when it was raining.

When I asked my mom about it, she told me to wait and see.

28

1. <u>Say</u> the word. <u>Trace</u> the word. <u>Write</u> the word.

her her

him him

2. <u>Read</u>. <u>Write</u> the missing word (**"him"**, **"a,"** or **"her"**).

My sister is a baby. I cannot help her. She needs her mother.

One day, a big dinosaur fell down from the sky. He was green. A note was attached to him. It said, "Hi, I am a dinosaur!"

3. <u>Circle</u> the **3** errors in the sentence. Write the corrections above each error.

My brother (does) not want (to) become (a) hero.

29

1. <u>Find</u> and circle or cross out the words.

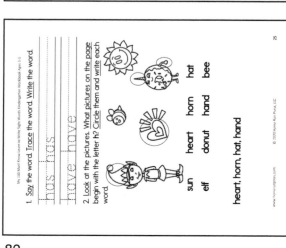

DAY   DOWN
EAT   EACH
EVERY   END
FIRST   FLY
FOR   FOUR
FROM   FIND
FUNNY   GET
GOOD   HAVE

30

1. <u>Say</u> the word. <u>Trace</u> the word. <u>Write</u> the word.

is is

in in

2. <u>Put</u> the fragment in the sentence.

My sister is good. At painting.

My sister is good at painting.

I discovered. A bright star in the sky.

I discovered a bright star in the sky. ☆

31

1. <u>Say</u> the word. <u>Trace</u> the word. <u>Write</u> the word.

it it

2. <u>Look</u> at the words and <u>think</u> about how they are related. <u>Find</u> the missing word in the list and write it.

out   am   it   front

he is to **is** as I is to _____   am

here is to **there** as in is to _____   out

John is to **he** as chair is to _____   it

after is to **before** as **back** is to _____   front

32

1. <u>Say</u> the word. <u>Trace</u> the word. <u>Write</u> the word.

into into

2. <u>Read</u> each sentence. <u>Write</u> the missing word (**"into"** or **"if"**).

My sister's puppy ran into my cat.

My cat could knock him if he wanted to.

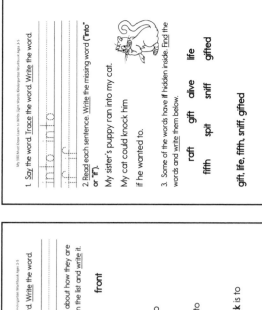

3. Some of the words have if hidden inside. <u>Find</u> the words and <u>write</u> them below.

raft   gift   alive   life

fifth   spit   sniff   gifted

gift, life, fifth, sniff, gifted

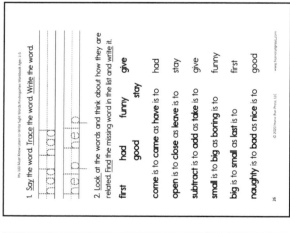

Card 33

1. Say the word. Trace the word. Write the word.

idea idea

its its

2. Read each sentence. Write the missing word ("idea" or "its").

I am something you create in your mind. I am an idea.

A bird couldn't find its egg.

3. Put the fragment in the sentence.

The frog put its head. Under the water.

The frog put its head under the water.

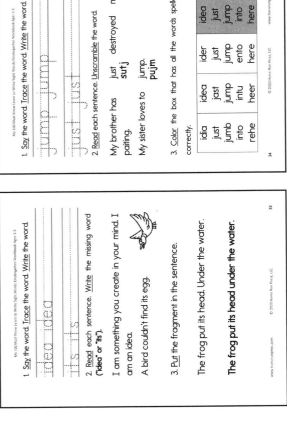

www.homerunpress.com   © 2020 Home Run Press, LLC   33

Card 34

1. Say the word. Trace the word. Write the word.

jump jump

just just

2. Read each sentence. Unscramble the word.

My brother has just destroyed my painting. **sutj**

My sister loves to jump. **pujm**

3. Color the box that has all the words spelled correctly.

idia	idea	ider
just	jast	just
jumb	jump	jump
into	intu	ento
rehe	heer	here

(shaded column): idea / just / jump / into / here

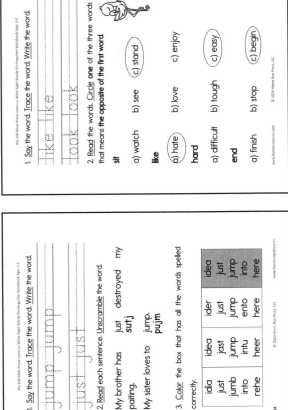

© 2020 Home Run Press, LLC   34

Card 35

1. Say the word. Trace the word. Write the word.

like like

look look

2. Read the words. Circle one of the three words that means the opposite of the first word.

sit

a) watch   b) see   c) stand

like

a) hate   b) love   c) enjoy

hard

a) difficult   b) tough   c) easy

end

a) finish   b) stop   c) begin

© 2020 Home Run Press, LLC   35

Card 36

1. Say the word. Trace the word. Write the word.

little little

long long

2. Use the code to write the word.

l = △   i = ○   t = □   e = ◇

△○□□△◇   little

a△ on ◇   alone

□ r ◇◇   tree

△ o v ◇   love

© 2020 Home Run Press, LLC   36

Card 37

1. Say the word. Trace the word. Write the word.

me me

my my

2. Read each sentence. Unscramble the letters.

What can I give to my
igve ym

Mom for Christmas?

A coloring book would be a nice icen
bkoo

gift.
tifg

You can get flowers, too.
nac etg

www.homerunpress.com   © 2020 Home Run Press, LLC   37

Card 38

1. Say the word. Trace the word. Write the word.

many many

more more

2. Find each word in the word search.

FIRST   JUST   DOWN   COME

BROWN   BLACK   DAY   FARM

END   LONG

```
B R O W N L O N G
H K C A L B D N E
D O W N K W H E T
S P T S R I F 8 Y
F A R M P Y U M A
E M O C Y J M S D
```

© 2020 Home Run Press, LLC   38

Card 39

1. Say the word. Trace the word. Write the word.

make make

made made

2. Read. Write the missing word ("make," "made," "many," or "more").

Verb tenses tell WHEN the *action takes place.*

Present tense expresses action or state in the **present time:**

I want to make this cookie.

Do you want more cookies?

Yes, I'd like more.

Past tense is what happened:

How many cookies did you have?

Last time, I made ginger cookies

www.homerunpress.com   © 2020 Home Run Press, LLC   39

Card 40

1. Say the word. Trace the word. Write the word.

may may

must must

2. Write the missing word.

MAY expresses a possibility.

Must expresses a strong certainty.

Pandas must live in places where bamboo plants grow.

Lions may sleep up to 20 hours a day.

A mouse may eat any kind of cheese.

Before you begin to exercise, you must stretch your muscles.

I must go to bed at 9 pm.

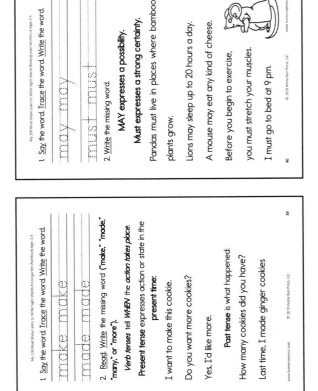

www.homerunpress.com   © 2020 Home Run Press, LLC   40

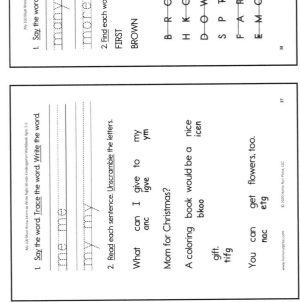

Page 41

1. Say the word. Trace the word. Write the word.

no no

not not

2. Color the clouds with the words that rhyme with **not**.

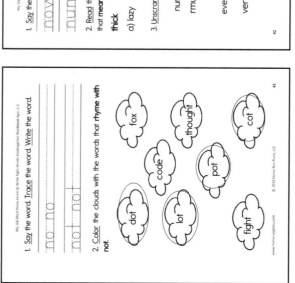

(clouds: fox, code, dot, lot, thought, pot, cot, fight)

Page 42

1. Say the word. Trace the word. Write the word.

now now

number number

2. Read the words. Circle **one** of the three words that **means the opposite of the first word**.

thick

a) lazy   b) tall   c) thin

3. Unscramble the words.

number	must
rmuneb	tums
every	make
verye	kema

Page 43

1. Say the word. Trace the word. Write the word.

name name

new new

2. Read the words. Circle **one** of the three words that **means the opposite of the first word**.

new

a) dirty   b) clean   c) old

3. Color the clouds with the words that **rhyme with name**.

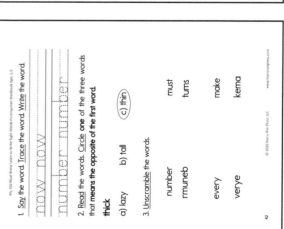

(clouds: blame, some, same, made, fame)

Page 44

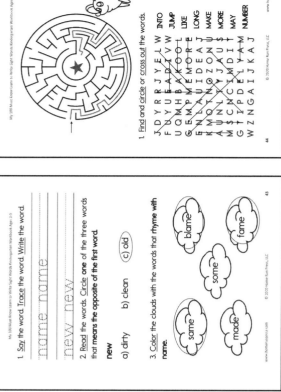

1. Find and circle or cross out the words.

```
J D Y R J Y E L W
F U Y U E A D I V W
U Q M H B A K O O L
G E M P M E M O R E
E K M O T N Q Z O N U
K M U N L T Y J A U S
M S C N C I M D I T
G T I P D E L Y A M
W Z N G A I J K A J
```

INTO		IDEA
JUMP		JUST
LIKE		LOOK
LONG		LITTLE MADE
MAKE		MANY
MORE		
MAY		MUST
NUMBER		NAME

44

Page 45

1. Say the word. Trace the word. Write the word.

off off

on on

2. Draw a line to connect the *synonyms*. Synonyms are words that have **the same or almost the same meanings.**

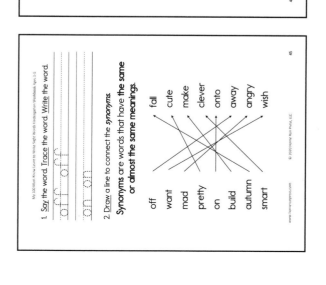

off	fall
want	cute
mad	make
pretty	clever
on	onto
build	away
autumn	angry
smart	wish

Page 46

1. Say the word. Trace the word. Write the word.

one one

our our

2. Write the **antonyms** in the blank

full	one	close	our
summer	**like**	**lost**	**ask**

their	_____
winter	_____
open	_____
found	_____
many	_____
empty	_____
answer	_____
hate	_____

Page 47

1. Say the word. Trace the word. Write the word.

old old

out out

2. Write the missing words ("old," "out," "on," "off," "of," and "inside").

Pumpkin carving is an **old** but enjoyable activity. Spread a piece of paper **out on** a table. Draw a circle around the pumpkin's stem and a creepy face **on** your pumpkin. Cut **out** the lid and scoop all of the seeds **out of** the pumpkin. Cut **off** the face and place a candle **inside** your pumpkin

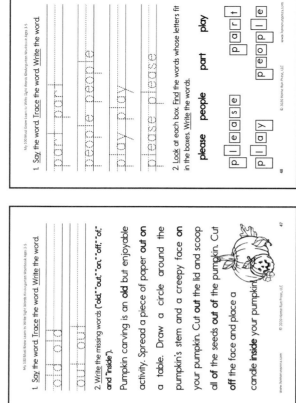

Page 48

1. Say the word. Trace the word. Write the word.

part part

people people

play play

please please

2 Look at each box. Find the words whose letters fit in the boxes. Write the words.

please   people   part   play

p|l|e|a|s|e   p|a|r|t

p|l|a|y   p|e|o|p|l|e

1. Use the words from the choice box to unscramble the words below.

part	alone	doctor	play
coat	cake	people	
key	**bike**	**people**	

cato — coat
lyap — play
rtpa — part
oelepp — people
iekb — bike
aoenl — alone
yke — key
crodot — doctor
ckea — cake

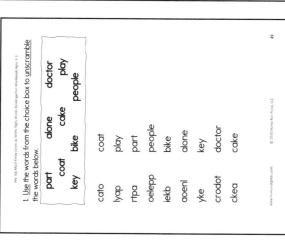

---

1. Say the word. Trace the word. Write the word.

red red
right right

2. Write the words in alphabetical order from a-z.

ran	1. after
make	2. ball
say	3. little
right	4. make
after	5. new
part	6. part
new	7. ran
little	8. right
ball	9. say

---

1. Say the word. Trace the word. Write the word.

ran ran
run run

2. Read. Write the missing word ("ran" or "run").

Bears do not like to **run**.

The rabbit **ran** with a blinding speed yesterday.

My cat **runs** and chases anything that moves.

Tigers are too big to **run** after the animals.

Last week, the foxes **ran** in circles to fool an enemy.

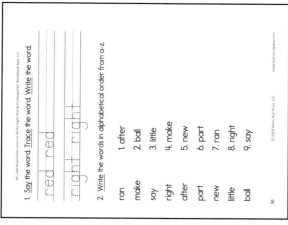

---

1. Say the word. Trace the word. Write the word.

read read
ride ride

2. Read the words. Circle one of the three words that means the opposite of the first word

right
a) good   (b) left)   c) back

read
a) help   (b) write)   c) bake

dark
a) full   b) soft   (c) light)

true
a) right   b) correct   (c) false)

---

1. Say the word. Trace the word. Write the word.

sad sad
she she

2. Say the word. Write the word, using the past tense of the underlined word in the first sentence.

caught   read   played

My sister likes to **read**.

Last time she **read** a fantasy book.

My cat loves to **play** with a ball.

Last time, it **played** with a ball.

A frog **catches** flies with its tongue.

Yesterday, a frog **caught** a fly with its tongue.

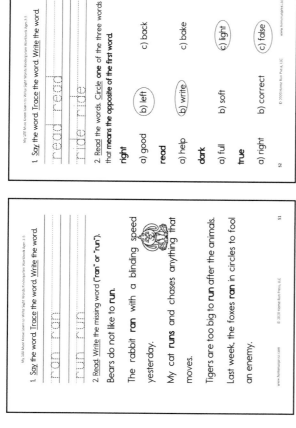

---

1. Say the word. Trace the word. Write the word.

so so
some some

2. Read the words. Circle one of the three words that means the same or almost the same as the first word.

home
a) field   b) lake   (c) house)

later
(a) then)   b) earlier   c) now

some
a) none   b) one   (c) any)

cold
a) hot   b) warm   (c) cool)

---

1. Say the word. Trace the word. Write the word.

see see
saw saw

2. Say the word. Write the word, using the past tense of the underlined word in the first sentence.

The dog cannot see clearly through his long thick hair.

I **saw** a snake and I was so scared!

Did you see my favorite book?

I **saw** mine under the table.

Can you see a star?

I **saw** a twinkling star in the sky.

I see a bird in the tree.

I **saw** one yesterday

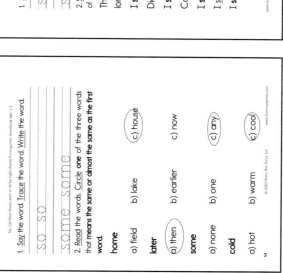

---

1. Say the word. Trace the word. Write the word.

say say
said said
the the
too too

2. Look at each box. Find the words whose letters fit in the boxes. Write the words.

tongue   sister   pretty   loves

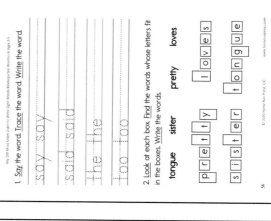

p r e t t y   l o v e s
s i s t e r   t o n g u e

Page 57

1. The words are mixed up. Rewrite each sentence in the correct order. Beware to use capital letters!

Capitalize the first word of the sentence!
Capitalize names and proper nouns!

sun is the big star a.

The sun is a big star.

has the to earth air breathe.

The Earth has air to breathe.

moon the no one on lives.

No one lives on the moon.

Page 58

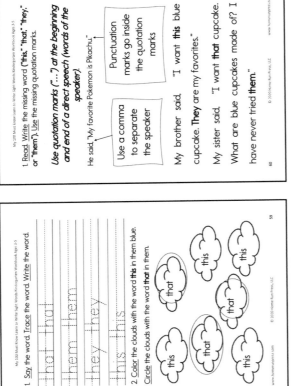

1. Find and circle or cross out the words.

E A D L P L R Q Y O	ONE	OTHER
X H A V X Z I Q U R	OUR	OLD
W S S P G O N E E R	PART	PEOPLE
R C Y H I K M D Z Q	PLAY	PLEASE
O L T P E O P L E K	RED	RIGHT
T W E K S T E E C X	RUN	SHE
H F N A A E R D X E	SAD	RIDE
E N U R S L W I Q A	SOME	SEE
R T R A P E P R L W		
O I F X Y T D N D Z		

Page 59

1. Say the word. Trace the word. Write the word.

that that ___
them them ___
they they ___
this this ___

2. Color the clouds with the word **this** in them blue. Circle the clouds with the word **that** in them.

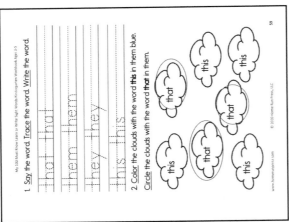

Page 60

1. Read. Write the missing word (**"this," "that," "they,"** or **"them"**). Use the missing quotation marks.

Use quotation marks ("...") at the beginning and end of a direct speech (words of the speaker).

[Punctuation marks go inside the quotation marks]

He said, "My favorite Pokemon is Pikachu."

[Use a comma to separate the speaker]

My brother said,   "I want **this** blue

cupcake. **They** are my favorites."

My sister said,   "I want **that** cupcake.

What are blue cupcakes made of? I

have never tried **them**."

Page 61

1. Say the word. Trace the word. Write the word.

their their ___
there there ___

2. Read. Circle the correct homophone.

Homophones are words that you spell differently but they sound the same and have different meanings

My friend is standing over their - there.

The scarecrow is standing over their - there house.

My bike's brake - break is broken.

My little sister likes to brake - break my toys.

I'm going to see - sea my Grandma.

See - Sea water tastes salty.

Page 62

1. Say the word. Trace the word. Write the word.

then then ___
three three ___

2. Draw a line to connect **homophones**. Say the words.

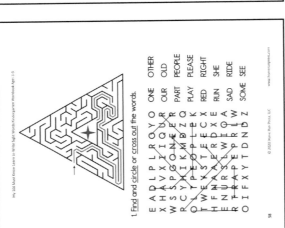

see	sun
here	tail
tale	poor
their	knight
right	our
night	sea
pour	hear
son	write
hour	there

Page 63

1. Say the word. Trace the word. Write the word.

than than ___
these these ___
time time ___
two two ___

2. Read each sentence. Practice writing the word.

There are some people who are over 8 feet tall. **These** people are called giants.

The **time** is 5:30 pm.

Two plus **two** equals four.

The chocolate cupcake is bigger **than** the strawberry cupcake.

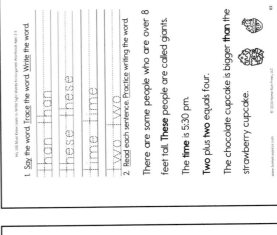

Page 64

1. Read each sentence. Circle if it is fact or opinion.

Fact can be proved to be true.

Ten is written as 10.

Opinion is what you think or how you feel about something

A fantasy book is the best Christmas gift.

The Sun is made of very hot gases.

The best place to live is near an ocean.

The Romans hd hundreds of gods.

Fact / Opinion

1. Say the word. Trace the word. Write the word.

up up

use use

2. Read each sentence.

Use *a question mark to end a sentence that shows a direct question. Use a period to end a telling sentence.*

When do skunks use their terrible smell?

A baby kangaroo hides in its mother's pouch after it is born?

How long can camels go without food or water?

Why do birds build nests?

Which insect has a sting in its tail?

Do elephants like to be in water?

65

---

1. Say the word. Trace the word. Write the word.

with with

word word

2. Read each sentence.

Use *an exclamation mark (!) to end a sentence that shows excitement.*

I am scared!

I love my new Pokemon card!

"Wow!" yells my sister.

I saw a twinkling star!

There is a mouse in my room!

Thank you for your Christmas gift!

Stop pulling my hair!

That's amazing!

Wow, look at that!

66

---

1. Say the word. Trace the word. Write the word.

want want

was was

we we

were were

2. Look at each box. Find the words whose letters fit in the boxes. Write the words.

father   mouse   want   mother

[w][a][n][t]

[m][o][u][s][e]

[m][o][t][h][e][r]

67

---

1. Read each word.

Circle *the pronouns (words that can take the place of a noun:* my brother = **he**).

Underline *the verbs (words that show action:* write, learn).

Write the words in alphabetical order from a-z.

(I)	1. am
want	2. he
(you)	3. I
(we)	4. it
am	5. say
was	6. she
(she)	7. use
(it)	8. want
use	9. was
say	10. we
(he)	11. you

68

---

1. Say the word. Trace the word. Write the word.

well well

went went

2. Read each sentence. Write the missing word ("well" or "went").

We went to the park.

My sister plays soccer very well.

3. Color the clouds with the word **well** in them yellow. Circle the clouds with the word **went** in them.

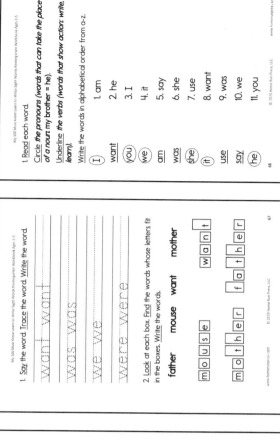

69

---

1. Say the word. Trace the word. Write the word.

what what

white white

2. Cross out all the lemons that don't show the word **what**. Circle all the lemons that don't show the word **white**.

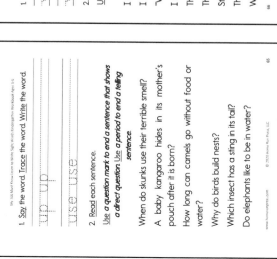

70

---

1. Say the word. Trace the word. Write the word.

when when

will will

2. Read. Write the missing word ("when" or "will").

When will you make a card for your friend?

The clouds will be made when many droplets of water are pushed together.

3. Circle the lemon with the word **when**.

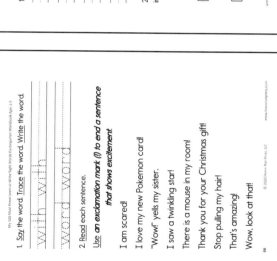
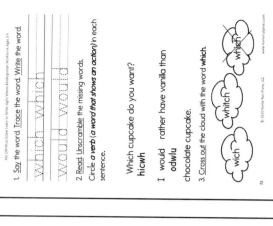

71

---

1. Say the word. Trace the word. Write the word.

which which

would would

2. Read. Unscramble the missing words.

Circle *a verb (a word that shows an action)* in each sentence.

Which cupcake do you want?

hicwh

I would rather have vanilla than odwlu chocolate cupcake.

3. Cross out the cloud with the word **which**.

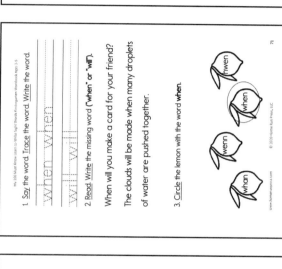

72

1. <u>Say</u> the word. <u>Trace</u> the word. <u>Write</u> the word.

who who

write write

2. <u>Use</u> the code to find out the word.

ß = w	Ō = i	£ = e
Â = t	Ø = o	∞ = h

n £ s Â   nest
∞ Ō l l   hill
ß ∞ Ø   who
ß £ £ p   weep
ß r Ō Â £   write
l Ō n £ s   lines
f l Ø ß £ r   flower

www.homerunpress.com   © 2020 Home Run Press, LLC

75

---

1. <u>Say</u> the word. <u>Trace</u> the word. <u>Write</u> the word.

yes yes

you you

2. <u>Write</u> the best antonym from the choice box.

yes	wet	tiny	full
	sick	stay	old
night			

day — night
empty — full
large — tiny
leave — stay
dry — wet
no — yes
well — sick
new — old

© 2020 Home Run Press, LLC   www.homerunpress.com

76

---

1. <u>Say</u> the word. <u>Trace</u> the word. <u>Write</u> the word.

water water

way way

2. <u>Unscramble</u> the compound word.

The **compound** word is formed when two or more words are put together.

otof + llab   **football**
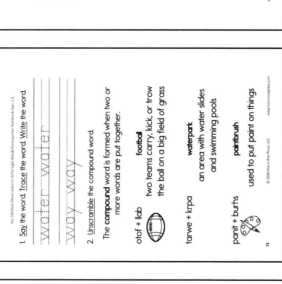
two teams carry, kick, or trow the ball on a big field of grass

tarwe + krpa   **waterpark**
an area with water slides and swimming pools

panit + burhs   **paintbrush**
used to put paint on things

© 2020 Home Run Press, LLC   www.homerunpress.com

74

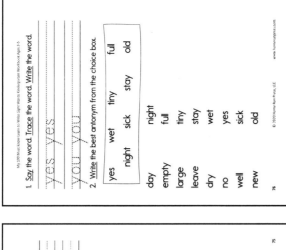

1. <u>Find</u> and <u>circle</u> or <u>cross out</u> the words.

```
W H I C H E U T Q I
Q Z N D O W S H X N
E E R H T S E E W A
B U W T E D I Y H W
L A M T C R O T E T
S E T H I O W H E N
Y H C T W N A H T
N Z Y G H I O A B S
W Y A G H I S W G Y I
W K J D B F S W V U
```

THIS   THEY
THREE   THESE
TIME   TWO
USE   THAN
WITH   WORDS
WANT   WAS
WHAT   WHITE
WHICH   WHEN

www.homerunpress.com   © 2020 Home Run Press, LLC

73

86